4

TURN UP
YOUR
FAT BURN!™

Weeks *to* FIT

Discover the Easy Way
to Burn Fat Fast!

The Editors of **Prevention** magazine

RODALE.

Portions of this book were previously published as *Turn Up Your Fat Burn!* by Rodale Inc. in April, 2011 and *Turn Up Your Fat Burn! Journal* by Rodale Inc. in April, 2011.

© 2017 by Rodale, Inc.

Printed in the United States of America

Rodale Inc. makes every effort to use acid-free ♾, recycled paper ♻.

Photographs by Mitch Mandel/Rodale Images

Library of Congress Cataloging-in-Publication Data is on file with the publisher.
ISBN-13: 978-1-63565-242-0

4 6 8 10 9 7 5   paperback

We inspire health, healing, happiness, and love in the world.
Starting with you.

Prepare for Maximum Fat Burn

THE EASIEST WAY TO BURN FAT FAST

Welcome to *Turn Up Your Fat Burn! 4 Weeks to Fit*. The 4 Weeks to Fit program is designed to help you achieve the fat-loss results you want. You probably already know the basic weight-loss equation: In order to drop excess pounds, you need to burn more calories than you consume. You can do this by drastically cutting calories; but for many of us, dieting alone is simply too hard. To get the best results, you also need to exercise. If you've been hitting the gym regularly and still aren't getting the results you want, it's time to improve your workout plan.

The secret is a metabolic marker called the Ventilatory Threshold 1 or VT1. This sounds complicated, but it's not. Honest! VT1 is the point during exercise when your body switches from feeding on carbs to converting fat stores to energy. Just before VT1, you're burning 51 percent fat, 49 percent carbs. The ratio then shifts, first to an even level, and then to 51 percent carbs, 49 percent fat. After the VT1 point, the ratio starts to shift more quickly, and you burn carbs at a much faster level.

With VT training, your goal is to raise your VT1 level so that you'll burn more calories overall and at the higher fat-to-carb ratio, which ultimately will help you lose weight more quickly.

How can you raise your VT1 level? Intervals. When you work out, you should alternate between a slightly higher intensity (briefly pushing your body to work just a bit beyond VT1) and a recovery period at a slightly lower intensity (staying at VT1 so that you are burning as much fat as possible). This will allow you to raise your overall VT1 levels after just a few weeks of training.

One study found that after a few months of training at and above VT1, subjects were able to shift their VT1 levels (and therefore burn more calories) by an average of 15 percent. That means a workout that used to burn 300 calories now burns 345! Another study found that women who exercised three times a week for an hour just above VT1 started to see a slight reduction in weight and BMI after just 2 weeks and a 6.2 percent difference in BMI after 8 weeks.

The more you train at and just above VT1, the more efficiently you'll burn fat. Best of all, when you teach your body to burn fat more efficiently, it starts to do that all day long—even when you're just hanging out. The average person burns only 4 to 6 percent of his or her weekly calorie intake through exercise, assuming three weekly sessions of 20 minutes each. But when the average man increases his VT1 level by as little as 10 percent, he'll burn 263 more calories daily—a pound of fat every 2 weeks, without even counting the workouts. The average woman will burn 178 more calories, which means an extra pound about every 3 weeks.

There's also a VT2 level, which is the point at which lactate and its by-products rapidly increase in your blood. You might hear some athletes refer to this as the lactate threshold. VT2 is the highest level of activity you can sustain (in well-trained individuals, it's about 30 to 60 minutes). At this point, you'll really "feel the burn"; that burning sensation is caused by the lactic acid and its by-products. But don't worry, you won't be seeing much VT2 training until your final week, when it's used as an extra challenge. The 4 Weeks to Fit plan concentrates mostly on VT1 training to increase your fat-burning metabolism.

LIFT WEIGHTS, BURN FAT

Most of us think of cardio as the only way to burn body fat. There's no arguing that you will reduce the most body fat if you incorporate aerobic training into your exercise routine. But resistance training also plays an important role in burning fat. In this program you'll be combining VT1 aerobic training and strength training to burn more fat.

There's a long list of benefits of strength training: helping build stronger bones, reducing blood pressure, lowering LDL ("bad") cholesterol, elevating HDL ("good") cholesterol, improving heart health, and even reducing the risks of diabetes and arthritis. But it's in the area of weight loss and weight maintenance that resistance training might have the biggest effect. Muscle plays a very important role in metabolism, or how your body burns calories. Muscle is more metabolically active than fat. Even at rest, muscle burns about twice the calories that fat does—roughly 7 to 10 calories for a pound of muscle, compared with 2 or 3 calories for a pound of fat.So the more muscle you have, the more calories you'll burn all day long.

Adding resistance training is especially important when you're trying to lose weight. Dieting alone will shift the numbers on the scale, but you'll be losing lean muscle mass along with fat. When you add weight training, you'll preserve and even build your muscle tissue while still getting rid of the fat. Think of it this way: For each pound you lose while dieting and *not* exercising, $^3/_4$ pound will come from fat mass and $^1/_4$ pound will come from muscle. When you diet and add strength exercise, you lose a full pound of fat while gaining an extra $^1/_4$ pound of calorie-burning muscle.

THE PROGRAM

The 4 Weeks to Fit program is designed to maximize your fat-burning ability by bringing together these two fitness fundamentals: an aerobic conditioning program that will elevate your VT1 level so you burn more fat with each workout and a strength routine that will boost your metabolism and keep you burning more fat all day long. Of course, the idea of doing both strength and cardio isn't new. But the key to getting results and helping you lose that extra fat lies in the way the workouts themselves are designed. Before you jump into the program, all you have to do is take a couple of quick tests to insure you'll drop those stubborn pounds fast. Make sure to utilize the journal starting on page 80 during the program so you get the most out of your workouts.

Finding Your Fat-Burning Sweet Spot

There's just one more thing you need to do before you dive into the 4 Weeks to Fit program, and that's determine your Ventilatory Threshold 1 (VT1), your fat-blasting sweet spot.

THE TALK TEST

The talk test is a well-regarded measure of exercise intensity. It's as simple as it sounds. You can fairly objectively determine how easy or hard you are exercising by how many words you can say without having to pause to take a breath. The talk test has been used for years by trainers and fitness pros to customize exercise intensity.

If while exercising you can go into full detail about the latest escapades in your office or go on a long rant about some family drama, you're probably moving at a low intensity. The harder you work, the more difficult it is to breeze through a conversation. If you increase your intensity to a moderately high rate, you can string together a few words or a short sentence without having to take a breath. Go at an all-out sprint and you probably won't be able to blurt out more than a syllable or two at a time. You also won't be able to keep up this intensity for very long.

Research shows that the talk test is closely tied to how fast your heart is beating and how much oxygen you are utilizing during exercise. The talk test also ties neatly into VT1.

At VT1, your body shifts from burning fat as your main fuel to burning more carbs. When your body is burning mostly fat, which for most of us is the primary goal, you can still speak fairly evenly and clearly. You can string together a couple of sentences and talk continuously for several seconds. At this level, you require more oxygen to burn the fat, but you're exhaling relatively little carbon dioxide. It's during the exhale that we talk, so your ability to speak isn't compromised. (Ever try talking while inhaling? Not easy.)

When you increase intensity with more speed or resistance (like an incline on a treadmill), you can still chat but can get out only a couple of short phrases at a time. Your cardiovascular system brings in more oxygen so your working muscles can do their thing. Your lungs have to push out the increased by-product of this respiratory process, carbon dioxide. You're breathing faster, and the more breaths you have to take, the harder it is to speak coherently.

That's why the talk test works so well for determining your VT1: It allows you to measure the point at which your body shifts from burning more fat to burning more carbs!

USING RPE

The rate of perceived exertion, or RPE, goes hand in hand with the talk test. RPE is another important way to determine your intensity during exercise. RPE ranks exertion on a scale of 1 to 10, with 1 being oh-so-easy (we're talking feet-up-on-the-couch territory) and 10 your absolutely maximum effort (sprinting-to-catch-a-plane hard).

Combining RPE and the talk test can help you figure out whether you should be walking or running a little faster, using a wee bit more resistance on a machine like a stationary bike or elliptical trainer, or increasing the incline a tad on the treadmill.

MONITORING YOUR HEART RATE

Determining your maximum heart rate is simple. Most formulas are too generic or simply too imprecise to help the average exerciser find his or her maximal rate. The most common formula, 220 minus your

Just How Hard Are You Working?

INTENSITY	RPE	FEELS LIKE	TALK TEST
No effort	1–2	Watching TV on the couch	Easy conversation
Very light	3	Window shopping	Easy conversation
Light	4	Walking to get somewhere	Very slightly breathless (mostly sentences)
Moderate	5	Walking to an appointment for which you're a little late	Slightly breathless (short sentences/phrases)
Moderately hard	6	Walking to cross the street before the light changes	Somewhat breathless (short phrases)
Somewhat vigorous	7	Late for a meeting with your boss/late for school pickup	Noticeably breathless (a few words at a time)
Vigorous	8	Very late for a meeting with your boss/very late for pickup	Noticeably breathless (a few words with difficulty)
Very vigorous	9	Late for a plane/running to get somewhere	Very breathless (hard to speak more than a word or two)
All-out effort	10	Sprinting to catch your plane	Can't speak

age, has been proven wildly inaccurate, because individual heart rates vary significantly among people of the same age. The results of this formula can be off by as many as 36 beats per minute. For a 30-year-old, the standard formula says the standard max heart rate is 190 beats per minute (220 – 30), but actually, it could be anywhere from 154 to 226 beats per minute.

VT training doesn't use heart rate to measure intensity, because it's more about breath rate than the number of times your heart beats per minute. So why bother with a heart rate monitor at all? The value lies in the objective measure of exercise intensity. Although RPE and the talk test offer insights into your intensity level, they are based on your own opinion of when an exercise feels challenging. A monitor offers an unbiased guide to intensity—the numbers don't lie. Having a set number to put with your talk test and perceived intensity can make it a little easier to determine your VT1 number, which will allow you to develop a more precise and effective training program.

DETERMINING YOUR VT1

Now that we've introduced some of the tools and guidelines, it's time to figure out your own VT1. One important note: Your VT1 can vary depending on the activity performed; some types of exercise are higher impact than others, plus you use different muscles and have a different center of gravity, all of which can affect your VT1. That means the number you get on the treadmill could be different from the one on the stationary bike, in part because on the treadmill, more of your upper body gets in on the action. You can still use different types of cardio during training, but for this test, choose the type of workout you think you will use most often during the next 4 weeks.

Your goal is to determine at what pace or intensity level you can no longer comfortably talk out loud without getting very breathless. So apologize in advance to the people around you if you work out in a public fitness facility, and get ready to go!

This entire test should take about 15 to 20 minutes. Ask a friend or training partner to write down the numbers you will be giving him or her. For best results, do the test twice, on two different days, and take an average of the results. This can help give you a better understanding of how to gradually increase your intensity and how your heart rate responds.

Step 1

Begin by warming up at a light effort for 3 to 5 minutes (RPE 3 to 4). This is your easy-conversation pace. If you're wearing a heart rate monitor, watch your heart rate level off, and stay there for at least a few minutes.

Step 2

Gradually increase your workload by small increments every couple of minutes (on a treadmill, increase each time by 0.5 mph or a 1 percent grade).

Feel good? Continue to increase the workload to a pace you feel you could maintain for a long period of time but makes you a little bit breathless. If you're wearing a heart rate monitor, watch for the number to level off, which should happen after about 30 to 60 seconds.

Here's the talking part of the test: Talk out loud for 20 to 30 seconds. You should be able to speak smoothly and continuously (not gasping for air but noticing when you have to take a breath).

Step 3

After the talk test, bump up the intensity slightly again, wait until your heart rate levels off, and repeat the talk test. Are you still able to speak smoothly and evenly? Continue to increase the intensity little by little, then repeat the talk test every couple of minutes, making sure your heart rate has leveled off each time before increasing the intensity.

Step 4

When speaking starts to become challenged (your words are choppy or forced out, but you're not gasping for air), you are at VT1.

If you're going to be training on the same machine throughout the program (and we recommend you do), keep note of your RPE and the speed and/or incline. If you're wearing a heart rate monitor, remember your BPM (beats per minute) at VT1.

Step 5

Continue to increase the intensity a few more times, increasing both RPE and breathing rate. Stay at each new level for at least 1 minute, allowing your heart rate to level off. Take note of your RPE, talk test results, and heart rate for each level. Stop when you get to the point when you can no longer say two or three words without having to take a breath.

It's important to keep going at least a little bit past your VT1 point so that you can have some idea of what it feels like to get more breathless during your intervals (and so you can avoid getting to this point in your weekly workouts on the program).

Step 6

Gradually start to cool down, until you are able to breathe easily and have an RPE of about 3 or 4.

Here's how this may play out for someone who is doing this test on a treadmill with 2-minute stages.

MINUTES	SPEED (MPH)/ INCLINE (PERCENT)	TALK TEST	RPE (1–10)	HEART RATE
0–5	2.5/1	Easy conversation (warmup)	3–4	117
5–7	2.5/2	Easy conversation	4	125
7–9	3.0/2	Slightly breathless	5	133
9–11	3.5/2	A little more breathless but can still speak in sentences	6	138
11–13	4.0/2	Words are choppy or forced (VT1 as determined by talk test)	6½	142
13–15	4.5/3	Difficult to say more than a few words	7	147
15–16	5.0/3	Difficult to say more than 1 or 2 words	8–9	155
16–20	3.0/0	Cooldown	3	120

How you structure your VT1 test (incline, speed, type of machine, or no machine) is entirely up to you. Just determine the point at which your breathing becomes choppy. Don't worry if your VT1 seems low—you're going to be working a bit above this level in your intervals. On the other hand, be honest about what seems difficult or how difficult it may really be to speak. If your numbers are too low, you won't be challenging yourself enough during the intervals to make a difference in your fitness level and raise your VT1 or fat-burning level.

Write down your VT1 level so you'll have it handy when you are doing the cardio intervals during the plan.

VT1 Test

MINUTES	SPEED (MPH)/ INCLINE (PERCENT)	TALK TEST	RPE (1–10)	HEART RATE

Before You Begin

If you haven't been working out regularly, starting a new fitness program can be a bit intimidating. With this plan, you won't be jumping into difficult routines right away. Over the next 4 weeks, your metabolic strength circuits and cardio VT1 interval routines will get progressively more challenging. In the Week 1 metabolic strength circuit, the focus is on basic strength moves like deadlifts, squats, lunges, and chest presses. For the cardio, you have a slightly longer recovery time than a work interval. In Week 2, the strength exercises become a little more challenging: now you'll start to combine moves, like adding a shoulder press to your deadlift or a triceps press to your squat. In the interval workout, work and recovery times are mostly equal.

In Week 3, you'll add in some jumping (plyometric) exercises to your metabolic strength workout to boost your heart rate, along with some balancing exercises to improve your sense of balance while also strengthening your core muscles. During the cardio, you'll have slightly less recovery time, compared with the work interval. And in Week 4, you'll add compound sets to your strength routine, working two exercises per muscle group with different types of movement. This final circuit routine will "shock" and strengthen your muscles in a whole new way, but after the previous weeks, you'll be ready for it. Meanwhile, we'll take the cardio intervals up another notch, this time getting close to VT2 for very short bursts of speed followed by recovery near VT1, which will challenge your aerobic fitness and help you achieve the results you want!

Begin your workout with the following warmup and dynamic stretches. Cool down with the static stretches.

Warmup: March or jog in place or go for a walk at a comfortable pace for 3 to 5 minutes. You should be able to maintain a conversation easily, but go fast enough that it doesn't feel like you're window shopping.

Then do the following dynamic stretches for about 30 seconds each, moving at your own pace. Keep the movements under control.

1 Knee Lift

Walk or march forward or in place, bringing your lifted knee to your chest. Try twisting gently to the opposite direction as you move (so if you're lifting your right leg, bring it toward the left as your torso twists to the right). Alternate sides.

② Butt Kicks

Walk or jog in place, bending your knees
to bring your heels toward your butt.

3 Frankenstein Walk

Slowly walk forward, lifting each leg straight in front of you to about hip height (or as high as you can comfortably go). Reach forward with your arms as you walk.

4 Cat-Back Stretch

a. Begin on your hands and knees. Round your back, contracting your abdominals and tucking your pelvis under.

b. Reverse the movement and arch your back like a cat, lifting your tailbone up and your chest forward while raising your head. Repeat the rounding and arching motions for 30 seconds.

1 Chest/Back Stretch

a. Stand with your hands behind your head, elbows out to the sides. Gently pull your elbows back as far as you comfortably can, arching your spine as you lift your chin, gazing up and feeling the stretch along your chest.

b. Keeping your hands where they are, bring your elbows together in front of your face, rounding your back and dropping your chin toward your chest, feeling the stretch along your upper back. Repeat the arching and rounding motions for 30 seconds.

STATIC STRETCHES

Finish your strength workout with a few static stretches to help increase your range of motion and speed your muscle recovery. Hold each stretch for about 15 to 30 seconds.

① Hamstrings Stretch

a. Stand with your legs together, then extend your right leg with your heel on the ground. Bend your left knee slightly.

b. Reach forward and grasp your right ankle or shin, keeping your right leg straight. Stretch your hamstrings and lower back by gently pulling toward your leg.

② Standing Quad Stretch

a. Support yourself by lightly holding onto a wall or chair with your left hand. Bend your right knee, grabbing your ankle behind you.

b. Gently pull your foot toward your butt; hold for 15 to 30 seconds, relax, and repeat on the opposite leg.

③ Calf Stretch

a. Stand facing a wall about 12 inches away from you. Take a big step behind you with your right foot, keeping both feet on floor and bending your left knee.

b. Lean into the wall, feeling tension along the right calf muscle. Hold for 15 to 30 seconds; switch sides and repeat.

④ Shoulder Stretch

a. Extend your right arm across your chest, your palm facing your body.

b. Gently pull your right forearm toward your body with your left forearm, feeling the stretch along the outside of your right shoulder. Hold for 15 to 30 seconds; switch sides and repeat.

⑤ Upper-Back/Chest Stretch

a. Interlace your fingers and extend your arms out in front, palms facing your body.

b. Drop your head and round your upper back; hold for 15 to 30 seconds.

c. Reverse the stretch, grasping your hands together behind you, palms facing your body; look up, arching your spine.

Week 1

Time to put all of your new knowledge about maximizing fat loss to good use. Welcome to the first week of the 4 Weeks to Fit training plan. Get ready to do some work, break a sweat, and—most of all—have fun!

YOUR GOALS THIS WEEK

○ Do two metabolic strength circuit workouts (about 30 to 40 minutes each).

○ Do two fat-burning cardio interval workouts (about 30 minutes each).

○ **Optional:** Do one moderate-pace cardio workout (about 30 minutes).

How you structure this program is entirely up to you. You can choose to do the strength and cardio on the same day or on different days. Just make sure you don't perform strength workouts on back-to-back days; you need to give your muscles time to recover and get stronger. You can add any other activities you like as long as you're still doing the prescribed cardio and strength workouts listed here.

Here's what a sample week might look like.

Monday: Metabolic strength circuit

Tuesday: Off

Wednesday: Cardio intervals

Thursday: Metabolic strength circuit

Friday: Off

Saturday: Cardio intervals

Sunday: Off or optional light cardio

How it works: Warm up by walking or jogging lightly for a few minutes and doing some dynamic stretching. Then start the strength circuit: Do the exercises in the order given, resting about 15 seconds between each move and a full 60 seconds at the end of the circuit. Complete the circuit three times. Do this workout two times this week on nonconsecutive days.

What you'll need: Light and medium weights, a sturdy chair or bench, and a mat (optional).

WARMUP AND STRETCH

March or jog in place or go for a walk at a comfortable pace for 3 to 5 minutes. You should be able to maintain an easy conversation, but go fast enough that it doesn't feel like you're out for a leisurely stroll.

Do the dynamic stretches starting on page 12 for about 30 seconds each, moving at your own pace. Keep the movements under control.

After the workout: Finish by doing the static stretches starting on page 17.

METABOLIC STRENGTH CIRCUIT
Week 1

This total-body strength circuit provides a strong foundation for your program. We're hitting all the major muscle groups here. Most of these exercises are fairly basic. You'll build upon each exercise as the program moves forward. For each exercise, use a weight that is heavy enough that your muscles feel like you've really worked them by the final rep.

So let's turn the page and get started!

① Romanian Deadlift

(works: hamstrings, glutes)

a. Stand with your feet hip-distance apart, holding medium weights in front of your thighs, palms facing your body.

b. Keeping your knees slightly bent and abs tight, hinge forward from your hips as you push your butt backward, slowly lowering the weights toward the floor. Squeeze your glutes as you stand back up. Repeat for a total of 12 to 15 reps.

FORM TIP! Make sure you feel the movement along the back of your legs (hamstrings), not in your lower back. Think of pushing your butt toward the wall behind you.

② Chest Press

(works: chest, triceps, shoulders)

a. Lie faceup on a step or bench. (If you don't have either, lie on the floor and position a large pillow or sofa cushion vertically under your back.) Hold medium weights at chest level with your elbows bent and your palms forward with wrists neutral (not bent).

b. Straighten your arms and press the weights above your chest. Pause, then slowly lower the weights back toward your chest. Do 8 to 10 reps.

FORM TIP! Don't bring your elbows too far down as you lower the weight (they should stop at about the same height as your chest); exhale as you straighten your arms.

③ Bent-Over Row

(works: upper back)

a. Place your left knee and left hand on a bench or sturdy low chair, holding a medium weight in your right hand with your arm extended directly under your shoulder. Keep your back flat and your head in line with your spine.

b. Draw your right elbow toward the sky, bringing the weight toward your ribs and keeping your arm close to your body. Continue to look down without arching your neck. Straighten your arm and repeat. Do 10 to 12 reps; switch arms and legs and repeat.

FORM TIP! Engage your abs by pulling in your belly button; keep your arm close to your body. You'll feel this more in your upper back than your arm.

4 Dumbbell Squat

(works: quads, glutes)

a. Stand with your feet hip-distance apart, holding medium weights at your sides.

b. Bend your knees about 90 degrees (or as far as you can) as if sitting in a chair. Stand up and return to the starting position. Do 10 to 12 reps.

FORM TIP! Keep your body weight over your heels and don't allow your knees to go too far forward—you should be able to see your toes if you look down.

Make it easier:
Do this exercise without any weight.

⑤ Standing Shoulder Press

(works: shoulders)

a. Stand with your feet a little wider than hip-distance apart, holding light or medium weights at shoulder height, your palms facing forward.

b. Straighten your arms and press the weights up, keeping your abs tight. Lower and repeat. Do 8 to 10 reps.

FORM TIP! Don't lock your elbows as you straighten your arms; try to keep your shoulders pressed down, not hunched up.

6 Stationary Lunge

(works: glutes, quads, hamstrings)

a. Stand with your feet hip-distance apart, holding medium weights at your sides, your palms facing your body.

b. Lunge your left leg forward, bending both knees 90 degrees and leaning forward slightly. Straighten your legs, keeping your feet planted, then bend your knees again. Do 12 to 15 reps. Switch sides and repeat.

FORM TIP! Keep your shoulders over your hips and your front knee directly above your ankle in the lunge; you should be able to see your toes if you look down.

⑦ Triceps Press

(works: triceps)

a. Hold two weights together above your head. (Option: Use just one slightly heavier weight.)

b. Bend your elbows and lower the weight behind your head. Straighten your arms and repeat. Do 8 to 10 reps.

FORM TIP! Keep your arms close to your ears as you lift and lower the weights.

⑧ Biceps Curl

(works: biceps)

a. Stand tall with your arms at your sides, your palms facing forward as you hold light or medium weights.

b. Curl your right hand toward your right shoulder, then lower your right arm as you curl your left hand toward your left shoulder. Continue, alternating arms, for a total for 8 to 10 reps per side.

FORM TIP! Use a full range of motion as you lift and lower the weight; keep your arms close to your body.

⑨ Plié Squat

(works: glutes, quads, outer thighs)

a. Stand with your feet just wider than shoulder-distance apart, toes turned out, holding medium weights in front of your thighs with your palms facing your body.

b. Pull in your abs to support your spine. Shift your hips back and down as you bend your knees 90 degrees, keeping your knees pointing in the same direction as your toes, your chest tall, and your abs tight. Squeeze your glutes as you return to the starting position. Repeat for 12 to 15 reps.

FORM TIP! Keep your knees tracking between your second and third toes; try not to allow the thighs to collapse inward.

⑩ Pushup
(works: chest, arms, abs)

a. Begin in a full pushup position, your hands on the floor and your legs extended behind you. Contract your abs and shift your weight forward so your shoulders are over your hands.

b. Slowly lower your body toward the floor, bending your elbows so your arms flare out slightly. Press back up to the starting position. Do 10 to 12 reps.

FORM TIP! Don't let your hips sag as you come down toward the floor; contract your abs to help maintain your form. If pushups hurt your wrists, hold a pair of dumbbells on the floor to reduce some of the stress.

Make it easier:
Do a modified pushup with your knees on the floor.

11 Plank

(works: abdominals, lower back)

Lie facedown on the floor, your elbows under your shoulders with your forearms on the floor, fingers facing forward, and legs extended with your feet about hip-distance apart. Lift your hips, forming a straight line from head to heels, keeping your abs tight. Hold here for 20 to 60 seconds.

FORM TIP! Don't allow your hips to sink or arch back. Hold only as long as you can maintain good form; if you need to take a break, rest and then repeat.

Make it easier:
Do the move from a full pushup position, your arms straight with your palms on the floor directly beneath your shoulders.

⑫ Bicycle

(works: abs, obliques)

a. Lie faceup with your lower back pressed into the floor, your hands behind your head with your elbows out to the sides. Bring both knees toward your chest, lifting your head, neck, and shoulders off the floor.

b. Lift your right shoulder toward your left knee while straightening your right leg. Switch sides, bringing your left shoulder toward your right knee. Continue for a total of 10 to 12 reps per side.

FORM TIP! Don't pull on your neck; think about bringing your shoulder rather than just the elbow toward the opposite knee.

FAT-BURNING CARDIO INTERVALS

Week 1

The 4 Weeks to Fit cardio plan includes 2 days each week of fat-burning intervals just above and below your VT1. Use the VT1 test on page 7 as a guide. If you wore a heart rate monitor (or used a pulse monitor) during that test, try to keep the work portion of your cardio intervals about 10 beats higher than your VT1. (So if you were at 145 for the test, work at about 155 here.) You can also go by the talk test; during the interval portion, you should be breathing heavily but not so hard that you can't speak at all.

You can do any form of steady-state cardio (an activity that gradually increases your heart rate and intensity and keeps you there), but for best results, stick with the same type of workout that you did for your VT1 test. That's because your VT1 level riding a bike or working on the elliptical trainer will likely be different than when you are running. We happen to like the treadmill best—it gives precise control over your speed, provides more cushioning than many outdoor surfaces like asphalt or cement, and allows you to adjust the incline to increase intensity if you don't like to jog.

Do this workout twice this week, either on the same day as your metabolic strength circuit or on an alternate day. You can also add a third (optional) cardio workout: a steady-paced, moderate-intensity activity (RPE 5 to 6) like brisk walking or bicycling for about 30 minutes.

MINUTES	EFFORT	TALK TEST	HEART RATE (OPTIONAL)	RPE
0–3	Light (warmup)	Easy conversation	Below VT1	3–4
3–6	Medium-high	Challenging (short phrases)	10 beats above VT1	7
6–10	Medium	Easier (short sentences)	Just below VT1	5
10–13	Medium-high	Challenging (short phrases)	10 beats above VT1	7
13–17	Medium	Easier (short sentences)	Just below VT1	5
17–20	Medium-high	Challenging (short phrases)	10 beats above VT1	7
20–24	Medium	Easier (short sentences)	Just below VT1	5
24–25	Light (cooldown)	Easy (full conversation)	Below VT1	3–4

Week 2

Welcome to Week 2! By now you should be feeling comfortable with the flow of the program and getting a feel for the routines. Hopefully, you're already starting to feel stronger and more energized. We'll continue this week with a menu of total-body workouts designed to make you leaner, fitter, and ready for action.

YOUR GOALS THIS WEEK

○ Do two metabolic strength circuit workouts (two or three times through; about 35 to 45 minutes per session).

○ Do two fat-burning cardio interval workouts (about 30 minutes each).

○ **Optional:** Do one fat-burning cardio interval workout (about 30 minutes).

Here's what a sample week looks like:

Monday: Cardio intervals

Tuesday: Metabolic strength circuit

Wednesday: Off

Thursday: Metabolic strength circuit plus optional cardio intervals

Friday: Off

Saturday: Cardio intervals

Sunday: Optional additional activity (golf, hiking, cycling, etc.)

Warm up by walking for a few minutes and doing some dynamic stretching. Then start the strength circuit; complete this workout two times this week on nonconsecutive days.

WARMUP AND STRETCH

March or jog in place or go for a walk at a comfortable pace for 3 to 5 minutes. You should be able to maintain an easy conversation, but go fast enough that it doesn't feel like you're out for a leisurely stroll.

Do the dynamic stretches starting on page 12 for about 30 seconds each, moving at your own pace. Keep the movements under control.

After the workout: Finish by doing the static stretches starting on page 17.

METABOLIC STRENGTH CIRCUIT
Week 2

This week we're building upon the exercises you learned last week, bringing the intensity up a notch. The moves are now a bit more challenging. You'll be working more muscles at the same time for a total-body workout that will boost your heart rate and give you a bigger postworkout afterburn. Stick with about the same weights you used for Week 1, but try to eke out two more reps for each exercise. If the dumbbells you chose last week felt too light, don't be afraid to challenge yourself a little and bump the weight up a bit.

This circuit takes a little longer and is more difficult; complete it at least twice, adding an optional third set depending on your time and energy level. Do the exercises in the order given, resting about 15 seconds between each move and a full 60 seconds at the end of the circuit.

What you'll need: Light and medium weights; a sturdy chair or bench; a paper plate, sheet of paper, or stability ball for the eighth move (bridge/hamstring curl); and a mat (optional).

Let's get started!

1 Romanian Deadlift with Shoulder Press

(works: hamstrings, glutes, shoulders)

a. Stand with your feet hip-distance apart, holding medium or light weights in front of your thighs, palms facing your body. Keeping your knees slightly bent and abs tight, hinge forward from your hips as you push your butt backward. Slowly lower the weight toward the floor, pushing your butt straight back toward the opposite wall, keeping your knees slightly bent and abs tight.

b. Stand back up and bring the weights to shoulder height, your elbows bent and your palms facing forward.

c. (not shown) Straighten your arms, bringing the weights together overhead. Lower your elbows back to shoulder height, and then bring the weights in front of your thighs. Repeat the deadlift/press combo for 12 to 15 reps.

FORM TIP! Hinge forward from your waist to complete the deadlift; don't lock your knees. You should feel tension in your hamstrings. Pause for a moment after you stand up, then do the shoulder press.

② Pushup with Row

(works: chest, triceps, core, upper back)

a. Begin in a full pushup position, hands holding light or medium weights on the floor under your shoulders and legs extended behind you, abs tight. Slowly lower your chest toward the floor, then straighten and repeat. Don't sink at the hips. Do 10 reps.

b. For the row, after your final rep, remain in the "up" position and lift your right hand, holding the weight. Bend your elbow, keeping your arm close to your body, lifting the weight until it's about even with your ribs. Lower and repeat. Do 8 to 10 reps, switch hands, and repeat.

FORM TIP! Remember to do all of the pushups first, then do the rows. During the rows, bring your feet wider apart to help keep you stable.

Make it easier:
Do a modified pushup with your knees on the floor. If this is still too difficult, you can do the pushup with your feet on the floor and your hands on a low counter or bench and do the row separately.

③ Alternating Lunge and Twist

(works: quads, glutes, obliques)

a. Stand tall, holding a medium weight horizontally in both hands close to your chest. Lunge your right leg forward, bending both knees.

b. Rotate your head, neck, shoulders, and torso to the right, keeping the weight at chest level while leaning your torso forward slightly. Push off your right foot and step back to the starting position. Repeat, lunging forward with your left leg and turning your upper body to the left. Do 10 to 12 reps per side.

FORM TIP! Keep your front knee over your ankle and your shoulders squared above your hips as you lunge.

Make it easier:
If you're having difficulty keeping your balance, just do the alternating lunge without the rotation.

4 Chest Press/Fly Combo

(works: chest)

a. Lie faceup on a step or bench. (Option: If you don't have a bench, lie on the floor and position a large pillow or sofa cushion vertically under your back.) Hold medium or light weights with your arms extended above your chest, palms forward. Slowly bend your elbows, lowering your arms out to the sides until your elbows are at chest level. Straighten your arms again.

b. Rotate your arms so your palms face each other. Slowly lower your arms out to the sides to chest level, elbows slightly bent. Lift the weights above your chest again. Repeat the press/fly combo for a total of 10 to 12 reps.

FORM TIP! During the fly (b) part of the move, move the weights in an arc that is in line with your chest; don't bring them too far forward or back.

5 Squat with Triceps Kickback

(works: quads, glutes, triceps)

a. Stand with your feet hip-distance apart, holding light weights next to your chest with your elbows bent behind you.

b. Push your butt back, bending your knees about 90 degrees (or as far as you can) as if sitting in a chair (you should be able to see your toes if you look down). As you lower down, press the weights behind you, keeping your arms close to your body. Stand up and return to the starting position, bringing your hands back toward your chest. Repeat the squat/kickback combo, doing 12 to 15 reps.

FORM TIP! Try not to arch your neck—keep your head in line with your spine—and keep your body weight over your heels. Start with your arms bent so that when you squat down, you straighten your arms and work your legs and arms at the same time.

6 Curtsy Lunge with Lateral Raise

(works: shoulders, quads, glutes)

a. Stand with your feet hip-distance apart, holding light weights with your arms at your sides, your palms facing your body. Cross your right leg behind you, as if in a curtsy, bending your left knee 90 degrees. Keep your left knee over your ankle.

b. As you bend your knees, lift your arms out to the sides to shoulder height, keeping your elbows slightly bent. Straighten your legs and lower your arms as you return to the starting position. Do 10 to 12 reps, switch legs, and repeat.

FORM TIP! Keep your knee aligned over your ankle and your shin vertical to the floor. Keep your torso upright and hips and shoulders as square as possible.

Make it easier:
Do the lunges and
lateral lifts separately.

7 Plié Squat with Heel Lift and Biceps Curl

(works: outer thighs, quads, glutes, calves, biceps)

a. Stand with your feet just wider than shoulder-distance apart, toes turned out, holding light or medium weights in front of your thighs with your palms away from your body. Bend your knees 90 degrees, keeping them in the same direction as your toes, with your chest tall and abs tight. As you bend your knees, curl the weights toward your shoulders. Stand up and lower the weights.

b. Rise up onto the balls of your feet for one count, keeping the weights in front of your thighs. Lower your heels and repeat the plié/lift /curl combo. Do 12 to 15 reps.

FORM TIP! Don't allow your knees to collapse in as you bend your legs; try pressing your knees out to the sides.

Make it easier: Take out the heel lift at the end of the move.

8 Bridge/Hamstring Curl

(works: hamstrings, glutes)

a. Lie faceup on the floor, knees bent with your heels on the floor, arms at your sides with your palms facing down. Place a paper plate or sheet of paper under your left foot. Engage your abs to stabilize your core and lift your hips, being careful not to arch your back. Hold for one count, then lower to the starting position and repeat. Do 12 to 15 reps.

b. On your final rep, keep your hips lifted. Slowly slide your left foot forward, keeping your hips steady and right foot in place, then slide your left foot back toward your body. Do 10 to 12 reps, then switch legs and repeat.

FORM TIP! If you have a stability ball, you can also do the bridge move with your feet on the ball and your legs straight, then use your heels to bring the ball toward your butt for the curl.

Make it easier:
Just do the hip lift and take out the hamstring curl.

⑨ Plank Combo

(works: abs, obliques)

a. (not shown) Lie facedown on the floor, your elbows under your shoulders with your forearms on the floor, fingers facing forward, and legs extended behind you. With your feet about hip-distance apart, flex your ankles so your toes are on the floor and your heels face the ceiling (see photo on page 30). Lift your hips, forming a straight line from head to heels, keeping abs tight. Hold for 15 to 20 seconds.

b. Rotate to the right side, lifting your right arm above your right shoulder. Keep your left forearm on the floor and turn it to face forward. Keep your body aligned and your legs stacked. Hold for 15 to 20 seconds.

c. (not shown) Lower for one count and switch sides, lifting your hips and rotating to the left as you lift your left arm above your shoulder, body aligned, and balance on your right forearm and stacked legs. Hold for 15 to 20 seconds.

FORM TIP! Keep your hips lifted and abs engaged throughout the exercise.

Make it easier:
Do the front plank (a) from a full pushup position, your arms straight. For the side plank (b and c), cross your top leg over your bottom one so both feet are on the floor.

10 Crunch Series

(works: abdominals, obliques)

a. Lie faceup on the floor, arms at your sides. Lift your legs above your hips. Holding your legs here, lift your head, neck, and shoulders off the floor, reaching your hands toward your feet. Do 15 to 20 reps.

b. Lower your upper body for one count, then reach your hands toward the outside of your left leg. Do 15 to 20 reps, then repeat, reaching toward the outside of your right leg.

FORM TIP! Keep a space the size of a tennis ball between your chin and chest; make the movement come from your trunk, not your neck.

Make it easier:
Bend your knees.

FAT-BURNING CARDIO INTERVALS

Week 2

This week we'll build on the intervals you did last week, making the intensity bursts a little longer while keeping the recovery time steady. Your work time is now just as long as your rest time. Try to make your work intervals just a little harder this week, bumping up your RPE by 1 point. On your heart rate monitor, aim for 10 to 15 beats higher than your VT1 during the intervals. This will help challenge you to work at a higher level, improving both your overall fitness and your VT1, while still giving you enough time to recover.

Remember, you don't want to work so hard that you're barely able to speak. During the work intervals, you should be able to quickly count to 15 (about 4 seconds) out loud without pausing to take a breath. Do this workout at least twice this week, adding an optional third session if you have time.

MINUTES	INTENSITY	TALK TEST	HEART RATE (OPTIONAL)	RPE
0–3	Light (warmup)	Easy conversation	Below VT1	3–4
3–7	Medium-high	Challenging (short phrases)	10–15 beats above VT1	7–8
7–11	Medium	Easier (short sentences)	Just below VT1	5
11–15	Medium-high	Challenging (short phrases)	10–15 beats above VT1	7–8
15–19	Medium	Easier (short sentences)	Just below VT1	5
19–23	Medium-high	Challenging (short phrases)	10–15 beats above VT1	7–8
23–27	Medium	Easier (short sentences)	Just below VT1	5
27–30	Light (cooldown)	Easy (full conversation)	Below VT1	3–4

Week 3

It's Week 3, which means you're halfway through the 4 Weeks to Fit program! We're continuing to build on the efforts made during the prior 2 weeks, adding more intensity to the strength workouts and making the cardio intervals a little more challenging. Keep up the good work!

YOUR GOALS THIS WEEK

○ Do two metabolic strength circuit workouts (two or three times through; about 35 to 45 minutes per session).

○ Do two fat-burning cardio interval workouts (about 30 minutes each).

○ **Optional:** Do one fat-burning cardio interval workout (about 30 minutes).

Here's what a sample week looks like.

Monday: Metabolic strength circuit

Tuesday: Cardio intervals

Wednesday: Off

Thursday: Metabolic strength circuit plus optional cardio intervals

Friday: Off

Saturday: Cardio intervals

Sunday: Optional additional activity (golf, hiking, cycling, etc.)

Begin with your warmup and stretch series. Then do the exercises in the order given, resting about 15 seconds between moves and a full 90 seconds at the end of the circuit. Complete the circuit at least two times through, doing an optional third circuit if time allows.

WARMUP AND STRETCH

March or jog in place or go for a walk at a comfortable pace for 3 to 5 minutes. You should be able to maintain an easy conversation, but go fast enough that it doesn't feel like you're window shopping.

Then do the dynamic stretches starting on page 12 for about 30 seconds each, moving at your own pace. Keep the movements under control.

After the workout: Finish by doing the static stretches on page 17.

METABOLIC STRENGTH CIRCUIT

Week 3

Now that you're halfway through the program and have done the strength circuits several times, we're going to increase the challenge again by adding on some balance exercises and plyometric (jumping) moves to build core strength and increase your calorie burn. If you can, you may also want to choose slightly heavier weights than you used the past 2 weeks. If you don't have heavier weights at home, add a couple of reps to what you did last week.

Remember to progress at your own pace. If a move feels too difficult or challenging to complete with the proper form, substitute a similar move from Week 1 or 2 (or just repeat either of those week's full circuits). Do this workout two times this week on nonconsecutive days.

What you'll need: Light and medium weights, a sturdy chair or bench, and a mat (optional).

① Lunge, Turn, and Lift

(works: quads, glutes, hamstrings, obliques)

a. Stand tall, holding a medium weight in front of your chest with both hands. Lunge your right leg forward, bending both knees (keep your right knee above your right ankle and your shoulders above your hips).

b. Rotate your arms, head, neck, shoulders, and torso to the right.

c. Step your left foot forward, lifting your left knee to hip height. Balance on your right leg for one count. Lunge forward with your left leg; repeat the series. Do 12 to 15 reps per side.

FORM TIP! Not a lot of room to move around? After you do the lunge/lift leading with your right leg, turn around and do the same move, this time stepping forward with your left leg.

Make it easier:
If balancing is difficult, bring your feet together and then lift your leg.

② Jumping Squat

(works: glutes, quads, core)

a. Stand with your feet hip-distance apart, your arms at your sides (no weights). Squat down, bending your knees about 90 degrees and keeping your weight over your heels (you should be able to see your toes if you look down).

b. Jump up, swinging your arms above your head, and land in a squat with your knees bent. Immediately jump again, landing in a squat. Do 15 to 20 reps.

FORM TIP! Land softly with your knees bent; move into the next squat as quickly as possible.

Make it easier:
If jumping doesn't feel good, do the dumbbell squat in Week 1, using slightly heavier weights.

3 Single-Leg Deadlift with Touchdown

(works: hamstrings, glutes, shoulders)

a. Stand with your feet together, your left hand holding a medium weight to your left side. Balance on your right foot, keeping your knee slightly bent.

b. Hinge forward from the waist, keeping your right knee slightly bent. Touch the dumbbell to the floor, bracing your abdominals; keep your torso parallel with the floor and your hips level. (You'll feel the movement along the back of your right leg.) Pull back up to start and repeat. Do 10 to 12 reps; switch sides and repeat.

FORM TIP! Keep your abs firm and your back straight to help with balance. Don't allow your torso to rotate.

Make it easier:
If balancing here is difficult, do a regular Romanian deadlift with both feet on the floor as in Week 1, using slightly heavier weights.

4 Balancing Alternating Biceps Curl

(works: biceps, core, glutes)

a. Stand tall with your arms at your sides, palms facing out and holding light or medium weights. Balance on your left foot.

b. Curl your right hand toward your right shoulder, then lower it as you curl your left hand toward your left shoulder. Continue, alternating arms, for a total of 8 to 10 reps per side. Then switch legs, balancing on your right foot. Repeat curls for another 8 to 10 reps per side.

FORM TIP! Help your balance by concentrating on a spot on the floor a few feet in front of you. Remember to switch legs halfway through the set.

Make it easier:
Keep both feet on the floor (or touch your foot down to the floor as needed).

5 Balancing Shoulder Press/Triceps Extension

(works: shoulders, triceps, core, glutes)

a. Stand with your feet together, holding light or medium weights at shoulder height, palms facing forward with your elbows in the 4 and 8 o'clock positions. Balance on your right foot, keeping the knee slightly bent.

b. Press the weights up, keeping your abs tight. Lower and repeat. Do 12 to 15 reps.

c. Switch legs, balancing on your left foot. Rotate your arms so that your palms face each other, keeping your weights close together above your head. Bend your elbows and lower the weights behind your head, keeping your arms close to your ears. Straighten and repeat. Do 12 to 15 reps. Then switch legs again and repeat the press/extension on the opposite sides.

FORM TIP! Keeping your abs pulled in can help you maintain balance. Remember to switch legs between the shoulder press and triceps extension.

Make it easier: Keep both feet on the floor (or touch your foot down to the floor as needed).

⑥ Scissor Lunge
(works: quads, glutes, calves)

a. Stand with your feet hip-distance apart, your arms at your sides (no weights). Take a short step (no more than 24 inches) forward with your right foot as if lunging, hinging your hips and lowering yourself toward the floor until your knees are bent about 90 degrees.

b. Explode up, switching legs in the air so you land with your left foot lunged forward. Immediately repeat, switching legs so your right foot is forward. Do 10 reps per leg.

FORM TIP! Don't lean too far forward when you jump, and land in a lunge position with your knees bent and your front knee over the ankle; use your arms for momentum.

Make it easier: If jumping is uncomfortable or too difficult, do regular stationary lunges as in Week 1, using slightly heavier weights.

⑦ Standing Halo

(works: core stabilizers, shoulders)

Stand with your feet hip-distance apart, holding one medium weight horizontally with your arms extended above your head, elbows bent. Slowly draw a big circle above your head with both hands, moving in a clockwise direction. Make 10 circles, then reverse directions.

Make it harder: Keep your feet together and/or make larger circles.

FORM TIP! Try to keep your torso and lower body still as you move your arms and shoulders.

⑧ Reverse Lunge with Double-Arm Row

(works: quads, glutes, calves, upper back)

a. (not shown) Stand with your feet hip-distance apart, your arms at your sides, holding medium weights. Lunge back with your right foot, bending both knees 90 degrees; keep your left knee above your left ankle.

b. Lean forward from your waist, keeping your back flat and abs engaged as you bring your chest toward your knees.

c. Draw both elbows past your ribs, keeping your arms close to your sides. Straighten your arms, then stand up, pushing off the left foot to step back to start. Do 10 reps of the lunge/row combo; switch sides and repeat.

FORM TIP! Keep your back flat and abs engaged as you lean forward from the waist to do the row.

Make it easier: If doing the lunge/row together seems too difficult, do the lunges with one side first, then hold on the final rep and do the rows; switch legs and repeat.

⑨ Step Up with Lateral Raise

(works: quads, glutes, outer thighs, shoulders)

a. Stand in front of a step, bench, or sturdy low chair, holding light weights at your sides. Place your left foot on the step or bench.

b. Step up with your right foot, bringing your arms out to the sides at shoulder height, elbows slightly bent. Step your right foot back to start while lowering your arms, then step down with the left foot. Repeat with opposite legs. Do 10 to 15 reps, alternating legs.

FORM TIP! Keep your elbows slightly bent as you raise your arms out to the sides, and engage your abs as you step up and down.

Make it harder: Add a balance challenge by lifting your back foot to hip height as you step up onto the bench.

10 Standing Torso Twist
(works: obliques)

a. Stand with your feet 6 to 12 inches apart, your hands in front of your chest, and hold a medium weight horizontally with both hands.

b. Rotate your upper body and head to the left as far as possible, holding for a moment without bouncing, then rotate back to center. Repeat, rotating to the right and back to center. Continue rotating left and right; do 15 to 20 rotations per side.

FORM TIP! Keep your lower body still and your hips facing forward throughout the exercise; the movement should come from your core.

⑪ Side Lunge with Kick

(works: quads, glutes, hamstrings, outer thighs, core)

a. Stand with your feet hip-distance apart, arms at your sides, holding light or medium weights. Step your left foot about 24 inches to the left side, keeping your weight over your heels and both feet facing forward. Shift your hips back as you bend your left knee 90 degrees. (Your right leg stays straight; most of your body weight is shifted into your left hip.) Lower the weights toward your left ankle.

b. Step the right foot forward to meet the left, and then kick your right leg powerfully to the side as you lean to the left; bring the weights toward your chest to help counterbalance. Lower your right leg and repeat. Do 10 lunge/kick combos; switch sides.

FORM TIP! During the side lunge, make sure your left knee is aligned between the second and third toes of your left foot and the shin is perpendicular to the floor. You should feel the movement along the left side of your butt. During the kick, you'll feel it along the right side of your butt.

Make it easier:
Take out the kick and just step feet together.

FAT-BURNING CARDIO INTERVALS

Week 3

Now that you're halfway through the program, it's time to increase the intensity of your cardio. This week, the "work" half of the interval is 5 minutes long, while recovery time is 4 minutes (1.25:1 ratio). Increasing interval length will help push your VT1, so you can burn more fat at a higher effort level (and ultimately burn more calories).

Your RPE during the work part of the interval should feel like 7 or 8 on a scale of 1 to 10—hard enough that your breathing is choppy but not so hard that you can't speak at all. Aim to keep your heart rate about 10 to 15 beats above VT1. Do this workout at least twice this week, with an optional third session.

MINUTES	INTENSITY	TALK TEST	HEART RATE (OPTIONAL)	RPE
0–3	Light (warmup)	Easy conversation	Below VT1	3–4
3–8	Medium-high	Challenging (short phrases)	10–15 beats above VT1	8
8–12	Medium	Easier (short sentences)	Just below VT1	5
12–17	Medium-high	Challenging (short phrases)	10–15 beats above VT1	8
17–21	Medium	Easier (short sentences)	Just below VT1	5
21–26	Medium-high	Challenging (short phrases)	10–15 beats above VT1	8
26–32	Medium	Easier (short sentences)	Just below VT1	5
32–34	Light (cooldown)	Easy (full conversation)	Below VT1	3–4

Week 4

You've made it to the 4th week of the program—congratulations! It may be the final week in this plan, but don't consider it as your final week of fitness. Think of this as simply the end of your first step toward a lifetime of better health and the beginning of a new journey of continued self-discovery.

By now we hope you've come to enjoy the experience and have started to notice some very real and lasting changes in your body and in your fitness and energy levels. After doing 3 full weeks of the plan, don't be afraid to take the intensity up another notch. It's rewarding to be able to challenge yourself and see what you're capable of. (Don't sell yourself short—you can do a lot more than you may think you can!) That said, please modify the plan as appropriate to make sure it works for you.

YOUR GOALS THIS WEEK

○ Do two metabolic strength circuit workouts (two or three times through, about 40 to 60 minutes per session).

○ Do two fat-burning cardio interval workouts (about 35 minutes each).

○ **Optional:** Do one optional fat-burning cardio interval workout (about 35 minutes).

Here's what a sample week looks like.

Monday: Metabolic strength circuit

Tuesday: Off

Wednesday: Cardio intervals

Thursday: Off

Friday: Metabolic strength circuit plus optional cardio intervals

Saturday: Optional additional activity (golf, hiking, cycling, etc.)

Sunday: Cardio Intervals

DYNAMIC WARMUP

This week we're departing from the usual warmup for a higher-energy routine. Do these exercises just once at the beginning of each workout this week, then immediately move on to the metabolic strength circuit on page 65.

After the workout: Finish with the static stretches on page 17.

1 Cat Back/Down Dog

a. Begin on your hands and knees. Exhaling slowly, round your back, contracting your abdominals and tucking your pelvis under. Hold for a moment.

b. Relax, then slowly inhale and reverse the movement, arching your back, lifting your tailbone up and your chest forward while raising your head. Hold for a moment.

c. (not shown) Return to the starting position on your hands and knees, with your spine neutral.

d. Lift your hips toward the ceiling, extending your arms and legs while pressing your heels toward the floor. Allow your head to drop between your arms. Hold for a moment; drop your legs and return to all fours. Repeat the entire series 5 to 10 times.

2 Bodyweight Squat and Arm Reach

a. Stand with your feet hip-distance apart, your arms at your sides (no weights). Squat down, bending your knees about 90 degrees or as deeply as you can, reaching your hands toward the floor.

b. Repeat, this time reaching your arms overhead.

c. On the next rep, reach both hands toward the left side.

d. On the next rep, reach both hands to the right side. Repeat the entire squat series (down, up, side to side), switching directions for the reaches with each rep, for a total of 10 series.

③ Around-the-Clock Lunges

a. Stand as if you're in the center of a big clock. Lunge your right foot forward (12 o'clock), then step back to center.

b. Lunge your right foot to the side (3 o'clock), then step back to center.

c. Lunge your right foot back (6 o'clock), then step back to center.

d. Lunge your right foot crossed behind you in a curtsy lunge (7 o'clock), then step back to center. Switch legs after you complete the series; do the series on each leg 5 times.

METABOLIC STRENGTH CIRCUIT
Week 4

This week you'll step up the intensity of your strength routine by working the muscles in different ways while also cutting back on your recovery time between each move. We're doing compound sets here, which means two exercises per muscle group. For the first exercise, you'll move primarily in a linear (up and down) movement; in the second, you'll add some rotation to work the muscles in a different way (and also bring other muscle groups in on the action).

Because the movements and exercises will be a bit more challenging, it's even more important to get your body ready for action. That's why we introduced the dynamic warmup moves you've just learned, which are designed to get you ready for the work ahead by boosting your heart rate and bringing your joints and muscles through a full range of motion. Do them just once.

After you do the dynamic stretches on pages 62–64, do the metabolic strength circuit two times through, this time resting for just 10 seconds between each move. Recover for a full minute between each circuit. If you have the time and energy, do a third circuit. Do this workout two times this week on nonconsecutive days.

What you'll need: Light and medium weights, a sturdy chair or bench, and a mat (optional).

1 Burpee (Pushup/Squat/Jump Combo)

(works: arms, chest, core, quads, glutes)

a. Begin in a full pushup position, your hands on the floor under your shoulders and your legs extended behind you, abs tight. Lower your chest toward the floor and push back to the starting position.

b. Jump both feet toward your hands.

c. Jump up, landing in a squat. Stand up and squat back down, then place your hands on the floor and jump your feet back to a pushup position. Do 5 push-up/jump/squat combos.

FORM TIP! Move through the exercise as quickly as possible, going from the pushup straight to the jump and squat. Land in the squat with your knees bent.

Make it easier:
If you have difficulty jumping, walk your feet back toward your hands, stand up and do a regular squat, then place your hands on the floor and walk your feet back until you're in a full pushup position. You can also do this as a modified pushup with your knees on the floor.

2 Decline Pushup

(works: chest, core)

a. Place your feet on a bench or sturdy chair and your hands on the floor in a pushup position, shoulder-distance apart.

b. Bend your elbows, lowering your head toward the floor. Straighten and repeat. Do 8 to 10 reps.

> **FORM TIP!** Keep your abs pulled in throughout the pushup to help maintain form.

Make it easier:
If the decline movement is challenging, do a regular pushup with your feet on the floor or a modified pushup with your knees on the floor.

3 Standing Dumbbell Fly

(works: chest, core)

a. Stand holding medium weights with your arms in front at chest height, palms facing each other, and your elbows slightly bent.

b. Slowly bring the weights out to the sides, keeping them shoulder height, then return to the starting position. Do 10 to 12 reps.

FORM TIP! Keep the weights at chest height; try to keep your shoulders pressed down and back, not hunched up.

4 Single-Leg Deadlift with Row

(works: hamstrings, glutes, upper back)

a. Stand with your feet together, holding a medium weight in your right hand at your side, your palm facing your body. Balance on your left foot, keeping your knee slightly bent. Hinge forward from your waist, keeping your left knee slightly bent and the weight directly under your right shoulder.

FORM TIP! Keep your arm close to your body and avoid rotating your torso; focus on a point on the floor to maintain balance.

b. Lift your right elbow toward your ribs, keeping your arm close to your body. Lower the weight, straightening your arm, then stand back up, staying balanced on your left foot. Repeat the deadlift/row combo 10 times; switch sides and repeat.

Make it easier:
If balancing is too challenging, do the exercise as a regular deadlift as in Week 1, adding in the row.

5 Reverse Lunge with Single-Arm High-Back Row

(works: quads, glutes, upper back)

a. Stand holding medium weights with your feet hip-distance apart, your arms at your sides. Lunge back with your right foot, bending both knees 90 degrees; keep your left knee above your left ankle. Lean forward, extending both arms below your shoulders, your palms facing your body.

b. Lift just your right elbow past your ribs, keeping your arm close to your body (your left arm stays down). Lower your right arm and step back to the starting position. Do 10 reps of the lunge/row combo; switch sides and repeat.

FORM TIP! As you lunge back, keep your shoulders over your hips, then lean forward for the row. Keep your head in line with your spine and your back flat during the row.

6 Single-Leg Squat with Heel Raise

(works: quads, glutes, calves)

a. Stand holding medium weights with your palms facing your body and your feet staggered, your left foot forward as if taking a step.

b. Hinge forward slightly from the hips, pushing your butt backward, then lower your hips toward the floor, keeping most of your body weight on your left leg. (You should feel your left leg muscles working.) Continue lowering until your front thigh is parallel (or nearly) to the floor. Keep your left heel pressed into the floor and lift your right heel. Pause for a moment, then push upward, standing back up.

c. As you stand, rise up on the ball of your left foot; hold for 1 or 2 seconds, then lower and repeat. Do 12 to 15 reps; switch sides.

FORM TIP! Keep most of the weight on your front leg as you squat down, getting as low as you possibly can, or until your thigh is parallel to the floor.

Make it easier:
If you find it too difficult to keep your balance here, do a regular squat, then raise both heels as you stand back up.

Make it harder:
Keep your back leg lifted throughout.

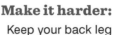

7 Biceps Blaster

(works: biceps)

a. Stand holding weights with your arms at your sides, your palms facing your thighs.

b. Curl the weights toward your shoulders, rotating your arms as you lift the weights so your palms face your shoulders. Reverse the movement and repeat. Do 8 to 10 reps.

FORM TIP! Move slowly and evenly, taking two counts to lift the weights and two counts to lower them.

8 Concentration Biceps Curl

(works: biceps)

a. Sit on a sturdy chair or bench holding a medium weight in your right hand. Lean forward, placing your left hand on your left thigh and bringing your right elbow just inside your right thigh, your arm straight.

b. Curl the weight toward your shoulder. Hold for one count, then lower and repeat. Do 8 to 10 reps; switch sides and repeat.

Make it easier: Use a lighter weight than you did for the previous exercise.

FORM TIP! Use your inner thigh to brace your arm for the exercise. Move your arm through its full range of motion, pausing briefly at the top.

⑨ Advanced Triceps Dip

(works: triceps)

a. Sit on the edge of a sturdy chair or bench, your hands at the edge of the seat with your fingers facing forward. Straighten your legs, keeping your heels on the floor in front of you.

b. Lift your hips off the bench and lower your butt toward the floor, bending your elbows directly behind you. Straighten your arms and repeat the dip. Do 15 to 20 reps.

FORM TIP! Keep your hips and body close to the bench or chair as you lower yourself.

Make it easier:
Bend your knees 90 degrees (keeping your knees over your ankles) during the dip.

10 Overhead Triceps Extension

(works: triceps)

a. Stand holding a medium weight in your right hand, with your right arm extended and your left hand lightly touching your right elbow.

b. Bend your right elbow, bringing the weight behind your head. Straighten back to the starting position and repeat. Do 10 to 12 reps; switch sides and repeat.

FORM TIP! Use your opposite hand to provide support and keep the elbow of your working arm still during the exercise.

11 Wood Chop

(works: quads, glutes, obliques, shoulders)

a. Stand holding a weight horizontally in front of you with both hands, with your right foot forward. Push your hips backward, then bend your knees into a squat. Rotate your hips and trunk to move the weight toward the outside of your right hip.

b. Press upward, rotating your hips and trunk while moving the weight diagonally across your body above your left shoulder. Repeat, lowering the dumbbell toward the outside of your right hip as you squat. Do 10 reps, then switch sides and repeat another 10 times.

FORM TIP! Move the weight diagonally from the floor toward the ceiling, with a full range of motion to work both your upper and lower body as well as your core.

Make it easier:
Do this exercise while kneeling.

12 Tabletop Twist
(works: obliques, glutes)

a. Begin with your shoulders on a step, bench, or sturdy low chair, your legs bent with your feet directly under your knees. Hold a weight in both hands with your arms extended above your chest. Keep your abs tight and hips level with your trunk.

b. Rotate your arms and torso to the left, lifting your right shoulder off the step until your arms are level with the floor. Pause for a moment, then rotate to the opposite side, keeping your hips elevated. Perform 15 to 20 reps per side.

FORM TIP! Keep your hips lifted and squeeze your glutes to keep your lower back from sinking.

FAT-BURNING CARDIO INTERVALS

Week 4

This week's cardio is a little different from the previous 3 weeks, when you primarily worked at and just above VT1. With this workout, you'll push past VT1 toward VT2—an even higher intensity level at which you will really feel the burn. This is a bit more of a butt-kicking workout, which makes it a good way to work on your overall fitness and wake up your body.

These speed intervals last just 20 seconds, so make them count: You'll get another 40 seconds to recover (although you'll still work at a medium-high intensity) before starting again. There are seven very high-intensity bursts altogether. If you're on a treadmill or other cardio machine, jack up the speed or resistance to a fairly high level (rather than gradually increasing it). Try to challenge yourself: Since the intervals are short, you want to make sure you're working at as high of an intensity as you can for a brief period. You'll continue to work at and above VT1 for a good portion of the workout, so you'll be burning plenty of fat along the way.

You'll be doing this workout at least twice this week, with an optional third session.

MINUTES	INTENSITY	TALK TEST	HEART RATE (OPTIONAL)	RPE
0–3:00	Light (warmup)	Easy conversation	Below VT1	3–4
3:00–13:00	Medium-high	Challenging (short phrases)	10–15 beats above VT1	7–8
13:00–13:20	Very high	Very challenging	15–20 beats above VT1	9
13:20–14:00	Medium-high	Challenging (short phrases)	10–15 beats above VT1	7–8
14:00-14:20	Very high	Very challenging	15–20 beats above VT1	9
14:20–15 :00	Medium-high	Challenging (short phrases)	10–15 beats above VT1	7–8
15:00–15:20	Very high	Very challenging	15–20 beats above VT1	9
15:20–16:00	Medium-high	Challenging (short phrases)	10–15 beats above VT1	7–8
16:00–16:20	Very High	Very challenging	15–20 beats above VT1	9
16:20–17:00	Medium-High	Challenging (short phrases)	10–15 beats above VT1	7–8
17:00–17:20	Very High	Very challenging	15–20 beats above VT1	9
17:20–18:00	Medium-High	Challenging (short phrases)	10–15 beats above VT1	7–8
18:00–18:20	Very High	Very challenging	15–20 beats above VT1	9
18:20 –19:00	Medium-High	Challenging (short phrases)	10–15 beats above VT1	7–8
19:00–19:20	Very High	Very challenging	15–20 beats above VT1	9
19:20–20:00	Medium-High	Challenging (short phrases)	10–15 beats above VT1	7–8
20:00–27:00	Medium High	Challenging (short phrases)	10–15 beats above VT1	7–8
27:00–32:00	Medium	Somewhat challenging	At VT1	5
32:00–35:00	Light (cooldown)	Easy conversation	Below VT1	3–4

Journal

Week 1

YOUR WEEK AT A GLANCE

DAY	WORKOUT	MINUTES
1	Warmup/dynamic stretches/strength circuit	30–40
2	Rest	
3	Warmup/dynamic stretches/cardio intervals	30
4	Warmup/dynamic stretches/strength circuit	30–40
5	Rest	
6	Warmup/dynamic stretches/cardio intervals	30
7	Warmup/dynamic stretches/cardio workout (optional)	30

What You'll Do This Week

2 × Metabolic Strength Circuit // 2 × Fat-Burning Cardio Interval
// 1 × Optional Moderate-Pace Cardio Workout

FIT TIP: It's no surprise that the harder you push yourself, the sorer you'll feel. So use this first week to gently ease into your program and learn to manage any aches. Doing some strength moves this week may in fact make you less sore when you do the full plan. If you do feel sore or a little achy after a workout, take some time to stretch. You can also take a nonsteroidal anti-inflammatory drug like Advil or Motrin to help with any lingering discomfort. (Be careful, as taking too many of these meds can lead to stomach, liver, or kidney problems; talk to your doctor if you have any concerns.)

Metabolic Strength Circuit Workout

Week 1

Do the exercises in the order given, resting about 15 seconds between moves and a full 60 seconds at the end of a circuit. **Complete the circuit a total of three times per session**. For more directions, training tips, and advice on how to perform these exercises safely, see pages 20–31. Don't forget your warmup and dynamic stretches.

What you'll need: Light and medium weights (heavy enough that your muscles feel fatigued by the final rep) and a sturdy chair or bench.

MOVE	WORKOUT 1 DAY/DATE: _____	WORKOUT 2 DAY/DATE: _____
Deadlift	Reps: _____ Weight: _____	Reps: _____ Weight: _____
Chest press	Reps: _____ Weight: _____	Reps: _____ Weight: _____
Bent-over row	Reps: _____ Weight: _____	Reps: _____ Weight: _____
Dumbbell squat	Reps: _____ Weight: _____	Reps: _____ Weight: _____
Standing shoulder press	Reps: _____ Weight: _____	Reps: _____ Weight: _____
Stationary lunge	Reps: _____ Weight: _____	Reps: _____ Weight: _____
Triceps press	Reps: _____ Weight: _____	Reps: _____ Weight: _____
Biceps curl	Reps: _____ Weight: _____	Reps: _____ Weight: _____
Plié squat	Reps: _____ Weight: _____	Reps: _____ Weight: _____
Pushup	Reps: _____ Weight: _____	Reps: _____ Weight: _____
Plank	Reps: _____ Weight: _____	Reps: _____ Weight: _____
Bicycle	Reps: _____ Weight: _____	Reps: _____ Weight: _____
CIRCUITS COMPLETED	1 ○ 2 ○ 3 ○	1 ○ 2 ○ 3 ○

Fat-Burning Cardio Intervals Workout

The 4 Weeks to Fit cardio plan includes 2 days a week of fat-burning intervals that work you just above and below your VT1. Try to keep the work portion of your cardio intervals about 10 beats higher than your VT1 (so if you were at 145 in the test, work at about 155 here). You can also use your talk test as a guide; during the interval portion, you'll be breathing heavily but not so hard that you can't speak at all (if you count out loud quickly, you should be able to get to 6 or 8).

Do this workout twice this week, either on the same day as your metabolic strength circuit or on an alternate day. You can also add a third (optional) cardio workout: a steady-paced, moderate-intensity activity such as brisk walking or bicycling for about 30 minutes.

What you'll need: You can do any form of cardio, but for best results with the intervals, try to stick with the same type of workout that you did for your VT1 test.

MINUTES	EFFORT	TALK TEST	HEART RATE (OPTIONAL)	RPE
0–3	Light (warmup)	Easy conversation	Below VT1	3–4
3–6	Medium-high	Challenging (short phrases)	10 beats above VT1	7
6–10	Medium	Easier (short sentences)	Just below VT1	5
10–13	Medium-high	Challenging (short phrases)	10 beats above VT1	7
13–17	Medium	Easier (short sentences)	Just below VT1	5
17–20	Medium-high	Challenging (short phrases)	10 beats above VT1	7
20–24	Medium	Easier (short sentences)	Just below VT1	5
24–25	Light (cool-down)	Easy (full conversation)	Below VT1	3–4

WORKOUT 1	WORKOUT 2	WORKOUT 3 (OPTIONAL)
Date: _____	Date: _____	Date: _____
Activity: _____	Activity: _____	Activity: _____
Length: _____	Length: _____	Length: _____
Work RPE: _____	Work RPE: _____	Work RPE: _____
Recovery RPE: _____	Recovery RPE: _____	Recovery RPE: _____

Week 2

YOUR WEEK AT A GLANCE

DAY	WORKOUT	TOTAL MINUTES
1	Warmup/dynamic stretches/cardio intervals	30
2	Warmup/dynamic stretches/strength circuit	35–45
3	Rest	
4	Warmup/dynamic stretches/strength circuit plus optional cardio intervals	60–70
5	Rest	
6	Warmup/dynamic stretches/cardio intervals	30
7	Optional activity (golf, hiking, cycling, etc.)	30

What You'll Do This Week

2 × Metabolic Strength Circuit // 2 × Fat-Burning Cardio Intervals // 1 × Optional Fat-Burning Cardio Intervals

FIT TIP: Go at your own pace! If you feel like you can't complete this week's workout without keeping the right form, it's perfectly okay to repeat the moves from Week 1. When you're ready, try the Week 2 moves. It's better to do a basic exercise correctly than to do a more complex one wrong.

Metabolic Strength Circuit Workout

Week 2

Keep the weights about the same as Week 1, trying to add two reps for each exercise. If the weights felt too light last week, don't be afraid to challenge yourself a little and bump up the weight a bit more.

Do the exercises in the order given, resting about 15 seconds between each move and a full 60 seconds at the end of a circuit. **Complete the circuit a total of two times** per session with an optional third set. Do two sessions this week on nonconsecutive days. For more directions, training tips, and advice on how to perform these exercises safely, see pages 35–44. Don't forget your warmup and dynamic stretches.

What you'll need: Light and medium weights; a sturdy chair or bench; a paper plate, sheet of paper, or stability ball for the eighth move (hamstring curl); and a mat (optional)

MOVE	WORKOUT 1 DAY/DATE: _____	WORKOUT 2 DAY/DATE: _____
Romanian deadlift with shoulder press	Reps: _____ Weight: _____	Reps: _____ Weight: _____
Pushup with row	Reps: _____ Weight: _____	Reps: _____ Weight: _____
Alternating lunge and twist	Reps: _____ Weight: _____	Reps: _____ Weight: _____
Chest press/fly combo	Reps: _____ Weight: _____	Reps: _____ Weight: _____
Squat with triceps kickback	Reps: _____ Weight: _____	Reps: _____ Weight: _____
Curtsy lunge with lateral raise	Reps: _____ Weight: _____	Reps: _____ Weight: _____
Plié squat with heel lift and biceps curl	Reps: _____ Weight: _____	Reps: _____ Weight: _____
Bridge/hamstring curl	Reps: _____ Weight: _____	Reps: _____ Weight: _____
Plank combo	Reps: _____ Weight: _____	Reps: _____ Weight: _____
Crunch series	Reps: _____ Weight: _____	Reps: _____ Weight: _____
CIRCUITS COMPLETED	1 ○ 2 ○ 3 ○	1 ○ 2 ○ 3 ○

Fat-Burning Cardio Intervals Workout

Week 2

Try to make your work intervals just a little harder this week, bumping up your RPE by about 1 point. On your heart rate monitor, aim for a number that's 10 to 15 beats higher than your VT1 during the intervals. This will challenge you to work at a higher level, improving both your overall fitness and your VT1, while still giving you enough time to recover.

Remember, you don't want to work so hard that you're barely able to speak. During the work intervals, you should be able to count to at least 8 (quickly) out loud. Do this workout at least twice this week, adding an optional third session if you have time.

What you'll need: You can do any form of cardio, but for best results on the intervals, try to stick with the same type of workout that you did for your VT1 test.

MINUTES	EFFORT	TALK TEST	HEART RATE (OPTIONAL)	RPE
0–3	Light (warmup)	Easy conversation	Below VT1	3–4
3–7	Medium-high	Challenging (short phrases)	10–15 beats above VT1	7–8
7–11	Medium	Easier (short sentences)	Just below VT1	5
11–14	Medium-high	Challenging (short phrases)	10–15 beats above VT1	7–8
14–18	Medium	Easier (short sentences)	Just below VT1	5
18–22	Medium-high	Challenging (short phrases)	10–15 beats above VT1	7–8
22–28	Medium	Easier (short sentences)	Just below VT1	5
28–30	Light (cooldown)	Easy (full conversation)	Below VT1	3–4

WORKOUT 1	WORKOUT 2	WORKOUT 3 (OPTIONAL)
Date: _____	Date: _____	Date: _____
Activity: _____	Activity: _____	Activity: _____
Length: _____	Length: _____	Length: _____
Work RPE: _____	Work RPE: _____	Work RPE: _____
Recovery RPE: _____	Recovery RPE: _____	Recovery RPE: _____

Week 3

YOUR WEEK AT A GLANCE

DAY	ACTIVITY/WORKOUT	TOTAL MINUTES
1	Warmup/dynamic stretches/strength circuit	35–45
2	Warmup/dynamic stretches/cardio intervals	30
3	Rest	
4	Warmup/dynamic stretches/strength circuit plus optional cardio intervals	60–70
5	Rest	
6	Warmup/dynamic stretches/cardio intervals	30
7	Optional additional activity (golf, hiking, cycling, etc.)	30

What You'll Do This Week

2 × Metabolic Strength Circuit // 2 × Fat-Burning Cardio Intervals // 1 × Optional Fat-Burning Cardio Intervals

FIT TIP: You don't have to grunt and groan with heavy dumbbells to see results. A study from McMaster University found that lifting light weights (about 30 percent of a maximum effort, or about 24 times until fatigue) was just as effective at building muscles as heavier ones (up to 90 percent maximum load, or about 5 to 10 reps before fatigue), as long as the person was able to fully fatigue the target muscle group by the final rep.

Metabolic Strength Circuit Workout

Week 3

Try using slightly heavier weights than the past 2 weeks. (If you don't have heavier weights at home, increase the number of reps from last week by another two counts or so.) If a move feels too difficult or challenging to complete with the right form, substitute a similar move from Week 1 or 2.

Do the exercises in the order given, resting about 15 seconds between moves and a full 90 seconds at the end of the circuit. **Complete the circuit at least two times through**, with an optional third circuit if you have time. Do this workout two times this week on nonconsecutive days. For more directions, training tips, and advice on how to perform these exercises safely, see pages 48–58. Don't forget your warmup and dynamic stretches.

What you'll need: Light and medium weights, a sturdy chair or bench, and a mat (optional).

MOVE	WORKOUT 1 DAY/DATE: _____	WORKOUT 2 DAY/DATE: _____
Lunge, turn, and lift	Reps: _____ Weight: _____	Reps: _____ Weight: _____
Jumping squat	Reps: _____ Weight: _____	Reps: _____ Weight: _____
Single-leg deadlift with touchdown	Reps: _____ Weight: _____	Reps: _____ Weight: _____
Balancing alternating biceps curl	Reps: _____ Weight: _____	Reps: _____ Weight: _____
Balancing shoulder press/triceps extension	Reps: _____ Weight: _____	Reps: _____ Weight: _____
Scissor lunge	Reps: _____ Weight: _____	Reps: _____ Weight: _____
Standing halo	Reps: _____ Weight: _____	Reps: _____ Weight: _____
Reverse lunge with double-arm row	Reps: _____ Weight: _____	Reps: _____ Weight: _____
Step-up with lateral raise	Reps: _____ Weight: _____	Reps: _____ Weight: _____
Standing torso twist	Reps: _____ Weight: _____	Reps: _____ Weight: _____
Side lunge with kick	Reps: _____ Weight: _____	Reps: _____ Weight: _____
CIRCUITS COMPLETED	1 ○ 2 ○ 3 ○	1 ○ 2 ○ 3 ○

Fat-Burning Cardio Intervals Workout

Week 3

This week, the "work" half of the interval is 5 minutes long, while recovery time is 4 minutes (1.25:1 ratio). Your effort level during the work part of the interval should be RPE 8—hard enough that breathing is choppy but not so hard that you can't speak at all. Aim to keep your heart rate about 10 to 15 beats above VT1. Do this workout at least twice this week, with an optional third session.

What you'll need: You can do any form of cardio, but for best results with intervals, try to stick with the same type of workout that you did for your VT1 test.

MINUTES	EFFORT	TALK TEST	HEART RATE (OPTIONAL)	RPE
0–3	Light (warmup)	Easy conversation	Below VT1	3–4
3–8	Medium-high	Challenging (short phrases)	10–15 beats above VT1	8
8–12	Medium	Easier (short sentences)	Just below VT1	5
12–17	Medium-high	Challenging (short phrases)	10–15 beats above VT1	8
17–21	Medium	Easier (short sentences)	Just below VT1	5
21–26	Medium-high	Challenging (short phrases)	10–15 beats above VT1	8
26–32	Medium	Easier (short sentences)	Just below VT1	5
32–34	Light (cooldown)	Easy (full conversation)	Below VT1	3–4

WORKOUT 1	WORKOUT 2	WORKOUT 3 (OPTIONAL)
Date: _____	Date: _____	Date: _____
Activity: _____	Activity: _____	Activity: _____
Length: _____	Length: _____	Length: _____
Work RPE: _____	Work RPE: _____	Work RPE: _____
Recovery RPE: _____	Recovery RPE: _____	Recovery RPE: _____

Week 4

YOUR WEEK AT A GLANCE

DAY	ACTIVITY/WORKOUT	TOTAL MINUTES
1	Warmup/dynamic stretches/strength circuit	40–60
2	Rest	
3	Warmup/dynamic stretches/cardio intervals	35
4	Rest	
5	Warmup/dynamic stretches/strength circuit plus optional cardio intervals	75–95
6	Optional additional activity (golf, hiking, cycling, etc.)	35
7	Warmup/dynamic stretches/cardio intervals	35

What You'll Do This Week

2 × Metabolic Strength Circuit // 2 × Fat-Burning Cardio Intervals // 1 × Optional Fat-Burning Cardio Intervals

FIT TIP: Dining out and not sure just how much or what you should be eating? Here's a simple way to figure out the right mix: Draw an imaginary peace sign on your plate. Fill the two large portions with fruits or vegetables. For the two smaller portions, fill one with protein such as chicken, seafood, or beef and the other with a grain such as lentils, chickpeas, or rice. If more food is pushed on you, fill your plate with more vegetables or fruit, and try to have fruit for dessert.

Metabolic Strength Circuit Workout

Week 4

This week you'll step up the intensity of your strength routine by working your muscles in different ways while also cutting back on the recovery time between moves. We're doing compound sets here, which means two exercises per muscle group.

Do the circuit two times through, this time resting for just 10 seconds between each move. Recover for a full minute between each circuit. If you have the time and energy, do a third circuit. Do this workout two times this week on nonconsecutive days. For more directions, training tips, and advice on how to perform these exercises safely, see pages 66–77. Don't forget your warmup and dynamic stretches.

What you'll need: Light and medium weights, a sturdy chair or bench, and a mat (optional).

MOVE	WORKOUT 1 DAY/DATE: _____		WORKOUT 2 DAY/DATE: _____	
Burpee	Reps: _____	Weight: _____	Reps: _____	Weight: _____
Decline pushup	Reps: _____	Weight: _____	Reps: _____	Weight: _____
Standing dumbbell fly	Reps: _____	Weight: _____	Reps: _____	Weight: _____
Single-leg deadlift with row	Reps: _____	Weight: _____	Reps: _____	Weight: _____
Reverse lunge with single-arm high-back rows	Reps: _____	Weight: _____	Reps: _____	Weight: _____
Single-leg squat with heel raise	Reps: _____	Weight: _____	Reps: _____	Weight: _____
Biceps blaster	Reps: _____	Weight: _____	Reps: _____	Weight: _____
Concentration biceps curl	Reps: _____	Weight: _____	Reps: _____	Weight: _____
Advanced triceps dip	Reps: _____	Weight: _____	Reps: _____	Weight: _____
Overhead triceps extension	Reps: _____	Weight: _____	Reps: _____	Weight: _____
Wood chop	Reps: _____	Weight: _____	Reps: _____	Weight: _____
Tabletop twist	Reps: _____	Weight: _____	Reps: _____	Weight: _____
CIRCUITS COMPLETED	1 ○ 2 ○ 3 ○		1 ○ 2 ○ 3 ○	

Fat-Burning Cardio Intervals Workout

Week 4

With this workout, you'll push past VT1 toward VT2—an even higher intensity level at which you are burning mostly carbs. If you're doing the workout walking or jogging outside, speed the pace to a jog or a sprint—it's only 20 seconds. You'll do this workout at least twice this week, with an optional third session.

What you'll need: You can do any form of cardio, but for best results on intervals, try to stick with the same type of workout that you did for your VT1 test.

MINUTES	EFFORT	TALK TEST	HEART RATE (OPTIONAL)	RPE
0–3:00	Light (warmup)	Easy conversation	Below VT1	3–4
3:00–13:00	Medium-high	Challenging (short phrases)	10–15 beats above VT1	7–8
13:00–13:20	Very high	Very challenging	15–20 beats above VT1	9
13:20–14:00	Medium-high	Challenging (short phrases)	10–15 beats above VT1	7–8
14:00–14:20	Very high	Very challenging	15–20 beats above VT1	9
14:20–15:00	Medium-high	Challenging (short phrases)	10–15 beats above VT1	7–8
15:00–15:20	Very high	Very challenging	15–20 beats above VT1	9
15:20–16:00	Medium-high	Challenging (short phrases)	10–15 beats above VT1	7–8
16:00–16:20	Very high	Very challenging	15–20 beats above VT1	9
16:20–17:00	Medium-high	Challenging (short phrases)	10–15 beats above VT1	7–8
17:00–17:20	Very high	Very challenging	15–20 beats above VT1	9
17:20–18:00	Medium-high	Challenging (short phrases)	10–15 beats above VT1	7–8
18:00–18:20	Very high	Very challenging	15–20 beats above VT1	9
18:20–19:00	Medium-high	Challenging (short phrases)	10–15 beats above VT1	7–8
19:00–19:20	Very high	Very challenging	15–20 beats above VT1	9
19:20–20:00	Medium-high	Challenging (short phrases)	10–15 beats above VT1	7–8
20:00–27:00	Medium High	Challenging (short phrases)	10–15 beats above VT1	7–8
27:00–32:00	Medium	Somewhat challenging	At VT1	5
32:00–35:00	Light (cooldown)	Easy conversation	Below VT1	3–4

WORKOUT 1	WORKOUT 2	WORKOUT 3 (OPTIONAL)
Date:	Date:	Date:
Activity:	Activity:	Activity:
Length:	Length:	Length:
Work RPE:	Work RPE:	Work RPE:
Recovery RPE:	Recovery RPE:	Recovery RPE:

Change it Up

After you finish the 4 Weeks to Fit program, continue the plan with these new metabolic strength circuits. You can do any of the moves individually or combine them to work several muscles simultaneously. Vary the focus so you're not working the same muscle group too many times in a row. Follow these simple guidelines when putting your metabolic circuit workout together.

Sample Circuit 1: At home (no equipment)

1. Bodyweight squat (quads, glutes)
2. Pushup (chest, arms, abs)
3. Around-the-clock lunge (glutes, quads, outer thighs, inner thighs)
4. Plank (abs, lower back)
5. Plank combo (abs, obliques, hips, shoulders)
6. Step–up and hold (quads, glutes)
7. Triceps dip (triceps)
8. Bridge (hamstrings, glutes)
9. Crunch series (abs, obliques)

Sample Circuit 2: At home, with dumbbells, single-focus exercises

1. Chest press (chest, triceps, shoulders)
2. Romanian deadlift (hamstrings, glutes)
3. Seated overhead press (shoulders)
4. Side lunge (outer thighs, glutes)
5. Lateral raise (sides of shoulders)
6. Concentration biceps curl (biceps)
7. Plié squat (glutes, quads, outer thighs)

8. Overhead triceps extension (triceps)

9. Standing torso twist (obliques)

Sample Circuit 3 : At home, with dumbbells, combo exercises

1. Pushup with single-leg raise (chest, shoulders, triceps, glutes)

2. Single-leg deadlift with row (hamstrings, glutes, upper back)

3. Squat with shoulder press (quads, glutes, shoulders)

4. Lunge with triceps kickback (quads, glutes, triceps)

5. Plié squat with heel lift and biceps curl (outer thighs, quads, glutes, calves, biceps)

6. Curtsy lunge with lateral raise (shoulders, quads, outer thighs, glutes)

7. Wood chop (quads, glutes, obliques, shoulders)

8. Plank combo (abs, obliques)

Sample Circuit 4: Balancing and plyometric exercises

1. Jumping squat (glutes, quads, core)

2. Balancing alternating biceps curl (biceps, core, glutes)

3. Scissor lunge (quads, glutes, calves)

4. Balancing triceps extension (triceps, abs)

5. Mountain climber (glutes, hamstrings, quads, abs)

6. Single-leg squat (glutes, quads, core)

7. Balancing overhead press (shoulders, core)

8. Burpee (arms, chest, shoulders, legs, glutes)

9. Single-leg deadlift (hamstrings, glutes, core)

10. Side plank (obliques, hips)

Sample Circuit 5: Balls and bands

1. Stability ball press (chest)

2. Stability ball fly (chest)

3. Seated row with band (upper back, biceps)

4. Standing row with tubing (biceps, upper and lower back, shoulders, core)

5. Ball squat (quads, glutes)

6. Bridge on the ball (hamstrings, glutes)

7. Ball curl (hamstrings)

8. Ball crunch (abs)

9. Tabletop twist on ball (obliques, glutes)

Sample Circuit 6: At the gym

1. Stability ball press (chest, triceps, abs)

2. Pullup or assisted pullup (upper back)

3. Seated row (upper back, biceps)

4. Triceps dip (triceps)

5. Seated overhead press (shoulders)

6. Lat pulldown (upper back)

7. Seated leg press (quads, glutes)

8. Standing leg extension (thighs, core)

9. Standing hamstring curl (hamstrings, core)

10. Standing hip adduction (outer thighs, glutes, core)

11. Standing torso twist (obliques)

12. Bicycle (abs, obliques)